# FROM SIDELINES

Inspired thoughts by Cheryl Ruettiger

This book was inspired from many thoughts and experiences raising my kids. I have always been the type of person who looks to make things better. One of my strengths is to improve upon things. I am a virgo after all lol. I always strive to make things perfect in an imperfect world which can be quite exhausting. But maybe I can at least make things better. I find some type of fulfillment and purpose in offering my own life experiences to develop a thoughtful template or way of doing things.

It seems I am always evaluating things, environments, situations, etc with so many thoughts whirling around in my head until one day all of them make sense, and come together in an applicable process that may make a difference in someone's life or in my own home town and beyond. I feel like we are all here to become the very best versions of ourselves. If we were all the very best version of ourselves or at least striving for that, then the world would be pretty epic.

# Thoughts and Refections

What if everything we did for someone else reflected to our lives somehow? What would our lives look like? What would the world look like? What if connecting to a positive energy connected us to the life we dream about? What if our mission in this life is to connect to that path? What if we actually are all connected and anything we do in the lives of others, we are actually doing for ourselves and at the same time elevating the universe?

"Your mind is a powerful thing. When you fill it with positive thoughts, your life will start to change."

Communication is a dance where the giver and the receiver must both contribute. What are the intentions of receivers? A coach communicates with a player and a player must communicate with the coach. There is not only a Giver. The Receiver must join in on the contract to give and receive for the greater good and change. The same is with a student/teacher connection. It's a contract that can be made at the beginning of each year and of course re-inspired along the way. It's an energetic contract. It's different than a contract where the giver expects nothing in return. Or when a gift giver gives a gift expecting a gift in return. It's not that. It's giving with a mutual understanding of the universal impact on how to make the giving and receiving work together to create greater good in both worlds. Everyone must do their part.

# Leaders Always Have Greater Responsibilities

When you're a coach or a teacher, you're accepting the responsibility to be a part of that child's life in a bigger way than just the sport or subject you're teaching. We can't assume that everyone gets the same things at home. It's definitely a service job that should be both an enjoyable and effective experience.

> "EVERY YEAR WE HAVE A NEW OPPORTUNITY TO LEARN AND GROW AND BECOME STRONGER LEADERS"

We have an opportunity to teach them self-love, the importance of reading, visualization and focus, character and integrity, patience and love, work ethic, training, persistence, and commitment, but not putting others down to raise ourselves up. We have to understand that we are all connected through a universal energy force - the spirit that lives within the physical body is an energetic force that everyone has. Everyone needs to know they can tap into that energy to become the best version of themselves.

We have an opportunity to help others see the best side of themselves. We can't focus on their insecurities and weaknesses. We have to bring out their strengths as a collective in the classroom, and on a team. It's about brotherhood bonding. It's about uniting for a common mission and a common goal.

One teacher and one coach can't do it all, but we can focus on what we have at the moment and on what we have each year - each class - each team. We can create a love that students and players will remember being a part of – Something that they can talk about and connect to. They will remember how great their coach and teacher was to them. They will realize that they can feel their best when they're with you, instead of fighting for attention or trying to prove themselves. That is just so discouraging and counterproductive in the end. This world is already hard enough. We all need a little space to grow and a little sunshine, and all of the elements that help us to feel good about who we are and who we can be. It's about hope, exploration, and possibilities.

It's about a confident next generation. It's about having them look at us and being proud of us. It's not a race. It's not a competition, even though it feels that way sometimes, especially when you're raising children. They're always feeling bad about something that someone said, did in school, or on the team, or someone who puts them down in order to raise themselves up.

We have to navigate those things and try not to give it power or participate in that type of energy. Because we know it's out there, we just have to get around it so we can grow. We get caught up in it to be accepted, to feel strong, to feel heard or to feel present. On a team, players FEEL the need to be chosen and to be an active player.

# Building a Team As One Collective Energy

What do you do with the players who aren't as athletically talented as the others? What do we do? That child is a part of the team. They are a part of the collective energy. Part of raising that team up is creating a unit to succeed and move forward. We have to deal with the things that we have in front of us.

Love and patience. I know kids think they have to win to be something great. I know that winning is perceived as being a reward of building a brotherhood and a bond. What makes winning important is when we win TOGETHER.

But, how do we do that while remaining true and authentic with each member of the team and considering various talent levels?

"A Leader always lifts someone up and focuses on their strengths, while encouraging them to keep going and growing"

Maybe it's about what we do off the field. Maybe it's about how we treat each other in the classroom and at practices. Maybe it's about those things. Maybe it's about letting that child feel that they're part of something great and that their friends are real friends, and that they are accomplishing something together during this block of time that they have together. Create an environment where they are all necessary parts of a winning team. This moment in time – this period in their lives will be significant as they look back and remember how you made them feel. It is important not to cast a shadow on them or make them feel isolated in any way. Through isolation comes many fears and anger and emotional disturbance. It's not up to us. We just have to do our best to be our best selves everyday, so that they too, can be their best selves everyday through inspiration, strength, and believing in the collective.

Give them something to love that loves them back. Everybody contributes. Playing someone's favorite song before practice to get hyped up and playing another person's favorite song at the end to close out the day or the practice. Make sure to close out in unity and strength. Close out by saying one great thing about another student or player. Create a circle. Create a bond. Say a prayer. Create a chant that unites the team. It will be something that identifies them as a team.

Create a team mantra that you say as a team or as a class before every practice and every game. Maybe each player or student adds one word to the mantra so that it represents everyone. People can have their personal mantras as well, but a team mantra is the collective mantra, the voice of the team.

Why doesn't everyone do that? I think because again everyone forgets about the perspective, the bigger picture, and what we are all really doing here. We forget why kids really need sports or why they really need a productive, loving classroom. Proper consideration of these concepts will change the world.

"A team is strongest when everyone does their part, feels like a valuable contributing member, and is working towards a common goal."

God is love and love is energy. Energy is a Life-Force. There's no denying that there is a force of energy inside of a physical being that makes it come alive. That energy is connected in the universe. It's not separate from one person to another. Without that Life-Force, we are just a body, a dead body that will deteriorate. We have to allow our spiritual side - our energy force to thrive. Feed it everything that's good and good will come out. The product will be good. We are spiritual beings having a human experience. Which reminds me to mention that we must also take care of our physical bodies. This will inspire our spiritual side so that we can be the best version of ourselves and also have the best spiritual experience. When you feel good then great things happen. You have better things to share with the people you are around everyday, most especially the kids you are leading on your team or in the classroom.

# Coach - Player Relationships

If you are going to put a kid on your team, he or she deserves an honest communication from the coach, as well as to know the coach's intentions regarding that player. If the coach plans to stack the team with "extra" players, then those players should be told that is their role. They should be told so they have an equal opportunity to decide if that is the commitment that they are willing and able to make. The process of broken promises and stringing kids along with a false hope is not reasonable and not acceptable and will breed resentment. There needs to be an upfront player/coach understanding of what is expected of them and their role on the team.

Communication and expectation is the important thing to focus on to have a productive team that knows their role, and can all move forward with a clear understanding of what is expected of them. There should not be more value placed on any one member of the team. It's about creating a unit that believes in each other. It would be a good idea to create a player/coach contract with the expectation that the contract can be revised at regularly scheduled coach/player meetings.

These changes can depend on the players performance and commitment to the current contract. This is a time when coaches can give players information about what they are doing well and what they can do better. It can also be a time when the player can discuss openly how their experience with the team is going. The point is to get rid of any toxic energy – energy that does not serve the team moving forward. Intentions and commitments should all be on the table upfront. It does not make sense to string kids along believing that they have a different opportunity then you intend to give them. Giving false hope is a sure way to breed discontentment, favoritism, and creates a situation that is discouraging to players expecting more than you intend to offer to them.

Possibly there is an optional plan for growth or training that could actually improve their skills and playing opportunities, but be careful with this if you are the person they are training with or if you benefit financially from their training. Coaches can get caught up in the wrong perception by benefiting financially from recommendations for their players.

Just keep things out in the open when it comes to financial opportunities. IF there are team fees or coaches fees they should be listed upfront and all players pay the fees equally in order to participate. Coaches should be compensated for their work the same as anyone with a job in any field of work. This should be expected by the participants so that fees can be out in the open and not viewed as some behind the scenes concealed revenue stream. This will create discontent with the players and their families which leads to mistrust and gossip.

"Build Teams that are Families and they will win not only on the field, but in the game of LIFE."

Maybe there is a trainer that you can refer kids to if they inquire about extra training on their own. If the coach is going to also do private training outside of team practices, it can lead to favoritism and a toxic situation. Parents who pay for extra private training with the coach can lead to some expectations regarding the play time for their child. It is probably best to have an outside trainer to refer your player to, someone who is not connected to your specific team and someone who does not decide the amount of playtime for each player.

Keep those things separate. Technically, players should not need outside trainers if team practices include the coach and assistant coaches all working together to cover the needs of each player /position and ultimately the team as a whole. Instead of paying for additional outside training, parents could then justify team fees and coaches fees that serve the needs of each player and offer skills training as a team.

# Player - Coach Contracts

Players should be able to trust their coaches to be honest with them and treat them with respect as a committed player and as a valuable asset to the team. It would be good practice for coaches to have player contracts for each player on the team, no matter how young or old the players are. It's a great way to introduce commitment by telling the players what is expected of them and the duties of their position on the team. This needs to be straightforward and honest so that players know what to expect.

The contract could include the following concepts and elements:

- Showing up for Practice
- Showing up for Games
- Being on Time
- Determine specific practice days/time each week
- Participating in Team Activitles
- Team Fees and Costs for the year
- Practicing good sportsmanship
- Being Kind
- Working Hard
- Respecting teammates
- Position on the Team
- Responsibilities of each position
- Games the player can count on being played, give specific dates
- Showing up even if you are not scheduled to play that game (This is for HS and up. In MS and younger all kids should get play time each game. This is an important part of their development)
- Team uniforms
- Dress codes for team activities
- Cell phone use
- Social Media Responsibilities
- Language - no profanity or down talk to others
- Book clubs to encourage reading – maybe (1) book per season. Meet and discuss along the way
- Discuss Safety

Schedule a contract review every month to make necessary changes, player promotions, recognitions etc. For example, if you have a player who is not a starting player, who shows marked improvement on the field/ice/court, who is also improving their skill level, this could create a positive situation for a contract revision. Possibly the coach can identify which games this player will be a starting player or get more time in the game, so that the player can notify family and friends to attend, most especially, on those dates to cheer on their *favorite* player and build positive energy all around.

I do want to make a point however that in the younger teams of youth sports before the later middle school years (grades 7-8), all kids should be played equally. By the time they reach the 8th grade, although I believe there should be more playtime here too, this can be more of a time for skill development and preparation for High School Sports.

"EVERY PERSON DOES THEIR PART. THAT IS HOW TO WIN AS A TEAM."

Building team bonding is just as important as building individual skills and elevating the skill level for the team as a whole. Kids or Adults who actually like each other and get to know each other, actually want to play well together. Play different kids in different positions, rotate different lines to see who plays best together – create a chemistry where the kids want to play well for each other – they want to win together – not to create a competition between players on the same team against each other – everyone counts and everyone is valuable – it's up to the coach to figure out the roles of each player based on their performance on the field. Help them build moments to interact with other players. Break down the walls that isolate kids. Give them a chance to grow and build skill levels to reflect their talent potential.

# PLEASE NOTE

Team Members should never be given the freedom to point out the mistakes of other team members. This is toxic and will break down team unity. Pointing out mistakes should **ONLY** come from the coach in a private positive exchange between the coach and that player. There are no inferior players. This is an opportunity for growth, not to condemn. If they are on your team then it is up to you to bring out their best.

Make a Master Schedule to include, practices, games, and team activities, meetings, etc. Make sure this gets distributed to every team member and their families so everyone can help make their player accountable. When we start habits like this when the kids are young, it becomes a part of who they are.

"EVERY YEAR WE HAVE A NEW OPPORTUNITY TO LEARN AND GROW AND BECOME STRONGER LEADERS"

For the Younger Kids, make sure the parents are a part of the contract meetings to help support everything at home and to avoid any misunderstandings. The coach should reach out to the parents ahead of time if there are any red flags or awkward discussions that need to happen during the contract and progress meetings. This is an important part of the child's development.

# Ideas for Team Activities

- Team 5K walks or runs for charity
- Team game watches for professional sports with pot luck at coaches house or contributing parent's house
- Outings to professional games
- Movie nights
- Escape Rooms
- Bowling
- Secret Santa during holidays
- Volunteer missions – teams sign up to help pack food for homeless teens and other volunteer programs
- Fitness Activities – Yoga class together – fitness classes – spin class etc.
- Mental Health Wellness activities – breathing exercises and meditation
- CPR classes
- Discuss Team tolerance for bullying
- Team Counseling Opportunities
- Guest Speakers for the Team
- Team Dinners
- Team Craft opportunities
- Game nights

# Continuing Education

Coaches should participate in annual accredited continuing ed classes for coaching and working with children. Including Safety training, CPR, Anti bullying classes, sexual and emotional harassment prevention etc. It would be a great idea to participate in classes that offer certification in a specific topic etc. This is super important and can justify a legitimate coach's salary as well. Being a coach is a huge commitment and responsibility and deserves a valuable salary, and at the same time requires huge accountability and patience with pure intentions to be your very best for the kids that you coach – both on and off the field. If this sounds like too much work to you, or if you prefer to play favorites, or just coach because your kid is on the team, then this job is not for you.

Create a team that stays together. Build that team each year to be stronger and stronger together. Some may leave due to life changes etc and new people will come, but the most important thing is a solid foundation to always operate from.

"CONTINUING EDUCATION ADDS VALUE AND INSPIRES COACHES & TEACHERS WITH FRESH EFFECTIVE IDEAS TO KEEP MOVING FORWARD"

# Maintaining The Day To Day

Coaches need to leave their baggage from the day at the door. The moment they walk onto the field they need to focus on the players and the team commitments. That's why a routine of warming up to a team song, chanting the team mantra, and choosing a player of the day are all great ways to recenter yourself from the day and focus on the moments in front of you

Rotating players to different positions keeps things fresh and also gives the coach a new perspective as to what is possible and the various talents of each player – at least for a portion of the practice, then shifting them to positions where each player holds the greatest strength for the second half of practice.

Build a family where the players learn to trust each other and be there for each other, work together – take egos out of the equation. It doesn't matter how long a kid has been playing a certain sport, each season is a new start and that definitely changes the dynamic and evens the playing field. Everyone enters the team as an equal and all must fulfill their player's contract by properly executing the plays and working in partnership with their teammates.

The stronger faster players will be someone that other players can look up to but not bow down to. It's important to keep everyone on the same emotional playing field reminding them that each player is a valuable part of the team. Remind each player of their strengths. Everyone makes mistakes. None of the players will be perfect and no one holds more value than anyone else. With that mentality you will build a solid team.

Because each player has a player's contract, it gives the coach an opportunity to make evaluations regarding each players performance and fulfillment of their player's contract. Coaches can make adjustments to the team based on these evaluations. The evaluations should be regular so that the players are tuned in to what they need to work on.

No bullying will ever be tolerated by anyone on the team. Depending on the intensity of the infraction, a penalty could be 1 warning with consequences. A second occurrence, and they are off the team. It's up to the coach to communicate this upfront and talk about the significance of this team rule.

Everyone counts and everyone is valuable. It's up to the coach to figure out the roles of each player based on their performance on the field. Help them build moments to interact with other players. Break down the walls that isolate kids. Give them a chance to grow and build skill levels to reflect their talent potential.

"TEAM BONDING IS THE HIGHEST PRIORITY. TEAMS THAT FIGHT TOGETHER WIN BIG!"

# The Influence Of Social Media

Coaches and teachers today have to deal with another level of interference called Social Media. Social Media can either make or break a kid's day. A misunderstanding on social media can distract the kids from what they need to focus on such as family, school, and their sport. It could also lead to validation struggles, deep depression, and a constant comparison of themselves to all of their peers who seem to be doing way better than they are. It is a good idea to have discussions about social media safety and the importance of putting everything into perspective. It is also important to let them know that they can always come to you about anything especially if they are in any kind of danger.

Some coaches may say that is not their job and that the families should be responsible for that. I agree that not one person can teach everything to someone, but if we have an opportunity to make a positive impact on the kids on our team, and do our very best with them for the time they are with us, then we have been successful, and the world is a better place at the same time.

It's okay to recognize a player for something even if they are not the best player. Maybe they are the most kind. That should go a long way in making them feel like a valuable appreciated part of the team dynamic. Not everything should be focused in a tunnel vision sort of way on just winning the game. If that is all there is, then there will definitely be a break down in the team connection and momentum. It takes each individual part to make a whole.

The times we remember as kids actually are not the amount of games that we won, but how we felt. How the coach made us feel is foremost. It is the most important thing. How the coach treats us is most likely how the other players will treat us as well. It all starts from the leadership. Being a good coach is a huge responsibility and should not be taken lightly. There are so many valuable opportunities to make a positive impact on these kids under our leadership. Keeping things transparent with team plans, schedules, opportunities, expenses, and coaches fees, will help to develop relationships of trust with the players, parents, and coaches.

# Team Managers

Having a great team manager can help to keep things organized and offer a reliable source of information so that all players and parents always have the info they need for a successful season. Team huddles should include the team manager and any assistant coaches. Assistant coaches should have a specifically defined job outlined as well.

They shouldn't be just random parent babysitters. They should be responsible adults who fit the team code. They should be able to support the value system that the coach has set for the team. There should not be any contradiction about how things are meant to operate. It's important for the coaching staff to be on the same page, operating under the same mission together.

Kids join sports teams for many reasons, not just because they like the sport, but also because they need to have a connection with friends and a common bond, with a common goal, to work towards.

"SUCCESSFUL TEAMS HAVE A CODE OF ETHICS AND CODE OF OPERATIONS"

# The Attitude Of Gratitude

The way I see it - anytime we are blessed to lead a group of children/teens, It's a time for growth, opportunity, and going to the next level. It's at time to allow more positive energy to flow into our lives and be a vessel to extend that energy on to others. Connecting with a positive energy source creates momentum for ourselves and for anyone within our circle. These are the things we need to share with those children on our team. You know, the kids grow up so fast and who they become is partly because of us. We can get so caught up in the day to day grind of life that we forget that things are going to change fast - pretty soon the kids we coach and teach in Middle School are going to be graduating college and starting careers.

Who they are will then have a huge impact on us, other families, communities, our society, and the world as a whole. We are all a part of the same system. That kid who is now grown up may become a coach or teacher for the next generation of kids. He or she will inevitably teach what they know and pass on what was passed on to them. I think the way to change the world is one person at a time – day by day. If enough kids are treated with love and respect as a child, then they will grow up to effect the next generation of kids in the same way. What we do each day matters. It definitely does.

"WHEN WE HAVE GRATITUDE FOR THE OPPORTUNITIES IN OUR LIVES, THEN WE ARE BLESSED WITH MORE OPPORTUNITIES"

# The Bigger Picture

Coaches, teachers, and parents are all a part of a bigger picture. When our kids are young, we think the only thing that matters is our child getting to play on the first string or getting enough game time. Sometimes we make their childhood all about that and lose focus on what is most important for their development. Coaches focus too much on just winning games without regard to the individuals involved. Winning is always exciting. If we can win by still taking care of each member of the team, then we truly win. We win by teaching them to care for each other and to support each other. We win by teaching them to build each other up and become like a family. Teams that become families win games and move on to win championships.

It's a consistent positive flow of energy that creates the momentum to win. I agree with parents that it is a huge self-esteem boost when the coach puts your child in the game. I do think that if the kid is invited to be a part of the team, then they should be given adequate opportunities to play as mentioned earlier. Some kids are not cut out for sports, but still need an opportunity to find out. They need honesty and communication – not just silence while they remain warming the bench day after day, and they definitely don't need to feel inferior in any way.

Coaches and Teachers – don't be afraid to communicate. It's everything. Truly. If you have kids in the classroom who are not contributing by showing up to class, getting passing grades, or understanding the course work, then it is time for additional communication. Each classroom should have a qualified teacher's aid or intern to help manage these things. Possibly, an assistant to manage the classroom communication and interactions with parents, when needed, is a good solution. It takes everyone – parents, teachers, coaches, etc to properly raise a child.

"Communication is a dance where both people must participate and contribute."

That is why continuing education for Parents, Teachers, and Coaches is necessary. Anyone in those positions should have a special certification to work with children on a daily basis. They are a part of this child's circle and influence them more than they know. It's just part of the territory. We can't expect just to wake up and work with kids. We need to connect to the right sources of knowledge, and inspiration to obtain the credibility we need to be successful.

On the field, it's more important to create better humans than to focus only on athletic skills. Not every player is meant to go professional. The ones that have that ability will be able to do that. If they do, we hope that they will also be great people, since at that point they will be in a very influential position where their behaviors and actions will be viewed by so many people – most especially the next generation of kids growing up. We all have responsibilities in our lives to be the best we can be – not only for ourselves but for others. Greater leaders will create greater communities and healthier kids.

"ALWAYS KEEP AN EYE ON THE BIGGER PICTURE - IT WILL HELP YOU FIND PERSPECTIVE IN ANY SITUATION"

Mental Health has been a major concern in our society over the past 10-20 years. The world today is full of people who overreact without thinking of the consequences. This is leading to destructive behavior and is destroying lives. The more we focus on leading kids with love, it will give them an opportunity to grow up in a better world and to become a generation that changes the course of the universe and provides an opportunity to have a healthy mental perspective.

# THE LIFE WE DREAM ABOUT

Is there a way to actually live the life that we dream about? Is there a way to connect to the positive energy source in the universe? If we, in our conscious mind, speak out loud the details of the life we would like to live, how do we get that to our subconscious mind so that we actually believe it? Once we believe it, is it then possible? If we do believe in a positive energy source in the universe – can we pray for the well being for others and specifically detail the healing for them that we are praying for… does that positive energy reach them and help them to connect with the potential to receive complete healing?

I definitely believe in connecting to the universal positive energy source to be able to radiate love and light in this world for ourselves and others. While we are physical beings on this earth, our life force is from the spiritual world.

Our bodies are the vessels for our life force – without our spirit, we are just functioning physical bodies. If this is what is true, then why wouldn't we want to connect to the spiritual positive energy force to heal the world, end all of the trauma, and significantly make an impact in the lives of the children growing up in this world. I believe that we can all make a positive impact on the bigger purpose of why we exist by focusing on becoming the best version of ourselves, and teaching the children to do the same.

Maybe not everyone will be aware of this positive energy life force for healing our spirits and our bodies, then we need to focus on the ones that are aware and tuned in to the opportunity. Keep shining the light bright. When we do this we make a difference in our own lives, the lives of someone else, and the universe. The light we shine gets brighter in the world. The brighter the light the stronger the positive force will be.

It is everyone's birthright to be happy and fulfilled. We are made from love and have free will to choose our path. When we focus on the life we dream about, we get closer to that life everyday. When we focus on the obstacles or problems, then our life is suddenly full of blocks that keep us from moving forward.

Even when we can not see the entire path ahead, we have to take one step each day – one thought, one connection, one behavior, one action that can change our lives. Fear of the unknown will try to defeat us. We have to keep moving. Changing our thoughts will change our actions, our behaviors, our habits – and this will change our lives.

"THE BEST WAY TO PREDICT THE
FUTURE IS TO CREATE IT"

# INSIGHTS FOR PARENTS:

THINGS I LEARNED ALONG THE WAY AND WISH I KNEW WHEN MY CHILDREN WERE BORN. MY HOPE FOR THEM IS TO BE ABLE TO IMPLEMENT ALL OF THESE THINGS NOW, AND WHEN THEY HAVE CHILDREN OF THEIR OWN.

## When Your Child is Born:

Set up a variable life insurance policy for 1 Million or more in their name. Don't wait. This should be in your child's name. Make the monthly payments. Payments are super low when your child is a few days old.

Set up a variable life insurance policy for 1 Million or more in your name while you are the youngest you will ever be. If we all had this set up when we were kids, the payments would be so much lower. Teach your kids this.

Set up a ROTH IRA – Contribute every month. don't wait. The younger your child is (day 1) the less expensive the payment and more time to grow.

Set up a high yield saving account and contribute any extra funds. This will be necessary for retirement or unexpected expenses.

In advance, arrange for cord blood storage to capture the cord blood at birth. This is essential for the health of your child and your family to have cells stored that can be accessed at any time during their lifetime. Identify their blood type.

Immediately take photos of the first day of life

Connect and bond with your child right away, setting up a healthy positive energy exchange with them.

Determine who will be a part of your child's circle and WHY. Define what each person's role will be and the impact they can make.

Create these circles and review them often to make sure the influence is what you need it to be.

Bond with your children everyday. Look them in the eyes when speaking with them. Breathe with them. Connect with them. It's important not to rush through life. It already moves fast enough.

Make self-care a priority! You need to feel good mentally and physically to offer your best self to your children.

Give yourself an opportunity to move your body daily – walks, gym, weights, classes, cycle, yoga, pilates, and more.

Inferred sauna or inferred light to keep the cells of your body charged and ready to replenish in a healthy way.

Cold plunge to energize, restore, reduce muscle or joint pains, to help increase metabolism or at least a 1 min cold shower at the end of your normal shower.

Massage and Stretching - reduces stress hormones and balances the body.

Design a go to diet to be able to access foods that will support a healthy lifestyle. Eat at home with whole real non-processed foods more than you eat out. Morning shakes or smoothies with proteins, vitamins, minerals, and adaptogens are super important. Eat more protein than carbs. Be sure to get a superior source of amino acids to build muscle and maintain a healthy metabolism. Vitamins C, D, B's, Omegas, magnesium and amino acids are super important for the healthiest foundation. I am certainly not a nutritionist and am only sharing insights I learned in my life along the way.

Sleep - make sure to give yourself 7-8 hours of sleep every night to feel rested, restored, recharged, and ready for the day ahead.

Stay focused in times of prosperity & growth as well as in times of depression. In times of growth we sometimes forget to be grateful. We forget to prepare for the times of depression when we have less income and opportunity. During these times we need to depend on any reserves we built during prosperity. Remaining grateful and setting some of our growth money aside can really help us to keep balance when things are harder. We can use times of prosperity to invest more for our kids and our futures, as well as get caught up on outstanding balances and chip away at our credit cards.

Make the relationship with your significant other a priority. Make sure to have date nights and build a bond that will be an inspiration and an example for children. It's Everything.

Maintain a source of Positive information as a foundation for your life. Happiness and Light is so important for positive brain development for your kids. This is even more important in a world that is filled with TV shows, Podcasts, Movies, Books etc where violence seems normalized – The things we surround ourselves with, in our world as a whole, is what shows up in our universe and becomes issues that we have to deal with in everyday life. We have to work hard to separate the fantasy from reality and remember that these things are not okay in our real world just because our world of "streaming services" is flooded with these thoughts and dramatizations. We need to focus on strong positive Mental Health development so that our children know what Is right, moral and ethical in our reality, and how other influences in the world of TV, books, and movies should not always be a normal part of our reality. Strong healthy kids full of love and faith is the goal we want to achieve. I would never want our children to have to live in a society that normalizes violence as a way to solve our problems. Positive mental health and Faith are necessary to raise healthy children and to contribute to the growth of a healthy high functioning society.

Create a circle of friends that are aligned with your energy and the types of people who you want around your children. Friends who make you feel valuable and who you feel good around. If you do not like who you are when you are around them, then get out of the friendship and move on. The best way to know if a partner or friend is good for you is to see how you feel ABOUT YOURSELF when you are around them. If you feel no confidence or not valuable or insignificant or less than you are, that is a sign that person is not for you.

# Discussing Mental Health

From my perspective, the root of all mental health is determined from how a person feels about themselves. How we feel about ourselves is very much linked to our life experiences beginning from birth. Our own self-worth is developed from how we are treated, the people we are around, our parents, our support system, our education, teachers, coaches, family dynamics, our opportunities, expression of our talents, communication, environmental influences, Interactions with Social Media, and other influences such as the music we are exposed to, the movies we watch, and how we engage with streaming services etc.

Somehow as we grow we need to find a way to sort through all of these things, and assimilate only the powerful useful information to find within ourselves the best way to arrive at our best selves. As young children we are like sponges just absorbing everything around us. Even in a troublesome environment, there can be people and interactions that can provide little sparks of hope that can lead us in the right direction. Inspiration can be like a magic force that can create change and make a positive impact on who a person becomes.

This is where teachers and coaches can be beyond valuable to the life of a child. We have a chance to make things better and spark a new path. We have an opportunity to introduce a new way of thinking and give them hope for the life they deserve and the goals they are meant to accomplish. We need to be the fuel to spark a passion that may have not yet been revealed.

Darkness breads more darkness, while light produces more light. A child who lives mostly in darkness needs access to the light to reveal parts of themselves that they never even knew existed, and to open up opportunities for greatness. I believe we are all capable of greatness. We just need to be presented with opportunities to expose that light, hopefully sooner than later in our lives, and at a time when we still believe that we have a chance to live the life of our dreams.

Sometimes even small gestures can make a positive impact on the mental health of a child, who lives mostly in the darkness and is constantly living in a pattern where every interaction breads more darkness. There are times when coaches and teachers can only see the darkness and are not offering any light because they can not see any willingness from the child to do better. This is when we should leave a little bit of light with a positive interaction, kind words, or a smile. These kind gestures can help break the pattern of darkness for that child and give them inspiration that will create change.

Leave something that will help open up the door of realization for that child. One time will not be enough, but it can help open the door. Another positive interaction from another willing person will open it further. Other positive moments in this child's life whether it be big or small with help give hope that maybe more is possible.

As leaders, we need to build on these moments for the kids that we are blessed enough to help influence. A source of light gives a child a chance to think that maybe they are worth it, and that maybe they do have value. This helps give them hope and realize that it is worth putting some effort into their goals and dreams, and ultimately believing they are capable.

When a child reaches a place where they start to believe in themselves, then they can begin to invest in themselves and realize that they can follow through on a coach/player or teacher/student "contract" to achieve more positive outcomes.

When a leader offers someone value, then everyone else will too. Earlier in this book we talked about creating contracts with our players and students to commit to team and classroom expectations. I am a strong believer in the concept of EVERYONE MUST DO THEIR PART.

When a child believes in themselves and has confidence and value, then they will WANT to fulfill their side of the contract. In order to help someone, they must first be willing to help themselves. Sometimes they just need help believing that they are capable.

A leader's behavior towards someone goes a long way. It makes a bigger ripple than we could ever possibly imagine. Take a chance to leave a positive impact every single time. It is ALWAYS worth it.

What happens to a child who lives in the darkness in a world of unsupportive people with zero positive sparks of hope? They could lose hope and become angry with a feeling of worthlessness. Their actions and behavior in this world could eventually lead to hurting themselves or others and living a life on a path of destruction. This is extreme, but represents the effects of how a life without love, value, and hope could lead to violence and destruction.

Leaders, teachers, and coaches have a chance to prevent a troubled life path for someone by taking the chance to do something good. Say a positive word, make a positive connection, and give someone a chance to WANT to do their part.

We can be the inspiration for others to be open to receiving help, and to want to be an active participant in their own lives and healing. Everyone deserves to be a work in progress and a masterpiece at the same time.

I want to refer to another quote to help gain insight into the thoughts I am sharing, "A rising tide raises all ships". It does! When we surround ourselves and others with positive ideas, energy, and a solid plan, everyone can benefit.

When everyone commits to a solid plan and knows their part in that plan, then we have the start of something awesome. We've then created a team of kids who want to work together, to fight for each other, to fail together, to build each other up, and to win together. They will win not only on the field, but also in the game of LIFE.

Everything we do matters. We can't be everything to everyone, but we can offer moments that will lead to other moments, and allow kids to recognize how they deserve to be treated. This will impact their entire life path. Because we can't be everything to everyone, we can offer resources for them like books, programs, counselors, and all things that will help build a stronger thread of value within kids who are not realizing these things for themselves, and who do not have the confidence to take a step each day towards something greater for themselves.

Giving a child hope and value will not only inspire them to want to work hard for themselves and their team, it will give them pride. The pride comes from them believing in their own abilities and hard work toward a common goal on a team or in the classroom. This will also lead to GRATITUDE because they are part of the equation for success. They are committing to something and working towards something.

They feel like a valuable and contributing member of the team. The contract will actually work because they are doing their part and following through. They now have a reason and are personally invested to the team and to themselves.

Call me a romantic, but I believe in a world where everyone has an opportunity to feel valuable, confident, and live their best life for the benefit of themselves and others, instead of at the expense of others. Everyone does their part. Let's all decide to level up so that our world can level up.

Positive mental health should be achievable to all children. It's up to us as the older generation to give our best to them, so that they can give their best for us. Self-love is an important part of living a valuable life. Our goal should be to help kids learn to love themselves and not give others permission to treat them in a degrading way. When we love ourselves, we know we are worthy of great things. All of this will be reflected in our behavior towards ourselves and to others. We deserve to see ourselves as the humble grateful king of our own lives and to treat others the way we want to be treated.

# COMMUNICATION AND CONFLICT RESOLUTION

Most things can be resolved through communication. As is true with the personal contracts mentioned earlier, "Everybody Does Their Part". Communication is also a partnership. The person speaking is not the only one who does the work. There must also be a listener who is just as committed to the conversation. The key to every conversation is awareness. Being aware in the moment and agreeing to be an active participant in the conversation is necessary for the one speaking and for the one listening.

It's important to engage in your role in the conversation, in order to understand what is being said. If you are the one speaking, the role of the listener will help create a calm environment for the speaker to be able to speak clearly. In this case the listener will have a better opportunity to understand the content of the speaker. It takes the active participation of both people to create an optimal environment to have a successful conversation. This definitely takes practice.

In the classroom or on a sports team it is okay to identify the role of each person when starting a conversation that involves an important point or issue that needs to be discussed or relayed to the listener.

For example, if a student approaches a teacher and would like to discuss an important issue, the teacher can identify their role in the conversation by letting the student know that they are listening. When the student has finished explaining their issue, the teacher can then say that it is now their turn to be the speaker. This will indicate to the student that their role now is that of the listener. It sounds pretty obvious when reading these words, but it does take practice to effectively engage in conversations to resolve issues etc.

Over time it will become a natural inclination to be both an effective speaker and an effective listener. You will be able to set the tone and the pace for every conversation that you are a part of just by being present in each role. Most times the other person will follow your lead. This can be a great way to keep things from going off course during a conversation. Sometimes intense emotions can elevate the conversation and when this happens the listener and the speaker can forget their role.

There will be interruptions and accusations, and misunderstandings if emotions get out of control. Try to re-center yourself during these times if you are the speaker or the listener. You can redirect the conversation once again just by taking a deep breath and remembering the end goal of the conversation is to understand what is being said, and to create an environment where the speaker can effectively explain their point, and the listener can clearly understand the speaker's point.

The end goal of a conversation is not necessarily to agree with the speaker, but to understand what they are saying. This is the first step in resolving any situation - to understand clearly what the situation is.

We all deserve the opportunity to live a fulfilling life. Let's use every opportunity we have, with the kids that we are blessed to teach and coach, to offer them many positive moments. The results will be a permanent part of who they are.

Through good times and tough times it's important to remember that life is dynamic and life situations will constantly change. We will have good days and bad days. If we are down, then the only way to go it up! Always keep moving forward so that you can be grateful for the good times and learn from the difficult ones. Keep moving forward every day, even if it is just one step at a time. Take one step every day and you will be on the right path.

Try these things during an attempt at conflict resolution in the classroom or on the field. These concepts will stay with the students for a lifetime and effectively make a difference in many conversations that they will have in their lifetime regarding important or difficult topics.

"Keep Going and Growing"

# Quotes from Famous Coaches

"Don't give up. Don't ever give up" - Jim Valvano, former N.C. State men's college basketball coach and national champion.

"It's not whether you get knocked down; it's whether you get up" - Vince Lombardi, former Green Bay Packers head coach and two-time Super Bowl Champion.

"Set goals - high goals for you and your organization. When your organization has a goal to shoot for, you create teamwork, people working for a common good" - Bear Bryant, former Alabama college football coach and six-time national champion.

"The key is not the will to win. Everybody has that. It is the will to prepare to win that is important" - Bobby Knight, former Indiana men's college basketball coach and Basketball Hall of Fame member

"Make sure that team members know
they are working with you,
not for you" - John Wooden

"Victory is in having done your best. If
you've done your best, you've won"
- Bill Bowerman, former U.S. track and field
coach.

"Success is peace of mind which is a
direct result of self-satisfaction in
knowing you did your best to become the
best you are capable of becoming"
- John Wooden, former UCLA men's
college basketball coach and 10-time
national champion.

"Our emphasis is on execution, not
winning" - Pat Summitt, former Tennessee
women's college basketball coach and
Basketball Hall of Fame member.

"What do you do with a mistake:
recognize it, admit it, learn from it,
forget it" - Dean Smith, former UNC men's
college basketball coach and two-time
national champion.

"There is nothing so uncertain as a sure thing" - Scotty Bowman, former NHL coachand nine-time Stanley Cup champion

"In basketball — as in life — true joy comes from being fully present in each and every moment, not just when things are going your way"- Phil Jackson, former Los Angeles Lakers and Chicago Bulls head

"Talent sets the floor, character sets the ceiling" - Bill Belichick, New England Patriots head coach and five-time Super Bowl champion.

"Champions behave like champions before they are champions" - Bill Walsh, former San Francisco 49ers head coach and three-time Super Bowl champion

"Discover your gift, develop your gift, and then give it away every day" - Don Meyer, former Lipscomb men's college basketball coach

"What keeps me going is not winning, but the quest for reaching potential in myself as a coach and my kids as divers. It's the pursuit of excellence" - Ron O'Brien, former U.S. diving coach responsible for 12 gold medals.

"The measure of who we are is how we react to something that doesn't go our way" - Greg Popovich, San Antonio Spurs head coach and five-time NBA champion.

"The greatest coaches aren't just game changers, they are life changers" -Tony Dungy

"I could not be more proud of the countless lives that I have changed since I began my coaching and mentoring career" - Dan Pena

"A good coach will make his players see what they can be, rather than what they are" - Ara Parseghian

"Hard work beats talent when talent doesn't work hard" - Tim Notke

"I've got a theory that if you give 100% all of the time, somehow things will work out in the end."
- Larry Bird

"Success isn't always about greatness. It's about consistency. Consistent hard work leads to success. Greatness will come"
- Dwayne Johnson

"We are what we repeatedly do. Excellence then, is not an act, but a habit" - Aristotle

"When you've learned to believe in yourself, there's no telling how good a player you can be. That's because you have the mental edge" - Rod Carew

"I don't think anything is unreasonable if you believe you can do it" - Mike Ditka

"Leadership is a matter of having people look at you and gain confidence...If you're in control, they're in control" -Tom Landry

"The best coaches never tell their athletes that they are wrong. They rather focus on creating awareness"
- Abhishek Ratna

"I've never felt my job was to win basketball games. Rather, that the essence of my job as a coach was to do everything I could to give my players the background necessary to succeed in life"
- Bobby Knight

"Good leadership isn't about advancing yourself. It's about advancing your team"
- John C. Maxwell

"Treat a person as he is, and he will remain as he is. Treat him as he could be, and he will become what he should be" - Jimmy Johnson, former Dallas Cowboys head coach and two-time Super Bowl champion.

"Do your best when no one is looking. If you do that, then you can be successful in anything that you put your mind to" - Bob Cousy, former Boston Celtics head coach and player and six-time NBA champion.

"The best teams have chemistry. They communicate with each other and sacrifice personal glory for the common goal"- Dave DeBusschere, former Detroit Pistons head coach.

"Be led by your dreams.
Not by your problems"
Roy Williams, UNC men's college basketball and three-time national champion.

"The difference between a successful coach and a great coach is the ability to inspire and empower their players"
-John Wooden

"Coaching's not a job, it's a privilege"
- Lee Corso

"Identify your problems, but give your power and energy to solutions"
- Tony Robbins

Keep this handbook with you at all times. It is a guide that can help you stay on track. There is more that you can add to this process based on your own knowledge, education, and life experiences. This is a template and a foundation to build on. This is a culmination of my experiences raising two children in sports and the performing arts. Life can be challenging with many unexpected situations that are out of our control. Breathe. Set yourself up for success ahead of time. No one expected 2020 to happen. In fact, everyone was excited for the new year until everything crashed. Everything changed – business closures, school closures, financial structure, our personal lives.

Have a steady plan and keep moving forward to be able to recover from various setbacks in our lives. There are many things that we can not control in our lives – we can only control our response to it and how we handle it. There will be a way. Be kind. Take care of yourself and your family. Project positive energy so that the world can receive it, and it can continue to heal and provide that same positive energy back to us.

# Contract Notes

Use the next few pages to create notes for your Coach/Player and Teacher/Student Contracts while the concepts are still fresh in your mind. It's important to also include your optimal Team and Classroom Goals to achieve effective results for both the individual students and players, along with the classroom and team as a whole. Use these pages to write some ideas to define your team mantra and identify the structure of a practice or daily operations in the classroom. Have fun and scribble away :)

Thank you for taking the time to read **From The Sidelines.** I hope these inspirations are helpful to you in building a successful team and classroom.

Made in the USA
Columbia, SC
18 November 2024

46421460R00054